The Misfits
and the
Rainy-Day Picnic

Dana Lynn Romero

Dedication

This book is dedicated in memory of my parents, Frank and Diane Romero, who always taught me to embrace my own quirkiness and that of others.

Acknowledgements

I would like to thank my amazing team at Amazon, Brian, Sarah, and Trevor, for all their hard work and diligence, in making this book a possibility. Thank you for your support and patience in bringing the Misfits to life. I look forward to working with you again soon as we take these friends on more adventures.

About the Author

Dana was born and raised in Southern California where she currently resides with her two sons, and a home full of animals. This is her first book in the Misfit series and is looking forward to bringing more adventures to life. She also writes romance novels.
When not writing, she works as a nanny, which she loves. In her free time, she can be found at the stables with her horses, antique shopping with friends, or crafting. "

IT WAS A BEAUTIFUL DAY IN THE GARDEN. THE MORNING SUN WAS PLAYING PEEK-A-BOO BEHIND THE WHITE AND GRAY CLOUDS. BRIGHT PINK TULIPS WERE IN BLOOM IN EVERY DIRECTION YOU LOOKED, AND YOU COULD SMELL THE FRESHLY CUT GRASS.

THE ONLY THING THAT COULD BE HEARD WAS THE SOUND OF CHUBS, THE CAT, RUSTLING THROUGH THE BUSHES AS HE LOOKED FOR GARDEN CRITTERS. BENJAMIN KNEW THESE CRITTERS WELL BECAUSE THEY WERE HIS FRIENDS. HE WAS PART OF A PLAYFUL AND ENERGETIC BUNCH OF MISFITS THAT LIVED IN THE GARDEN.

1

EACH DAY THEY WOULD HAVE AN ADVENTURE, AND TODAY WOULD BE A BIG ONE. BENJAMIN LOOKED DOWN FROM THE TREE BRANCH HE WAS STANDING ON. HE COULD SEE HIS FRIENDS IN THE GARDEN BELOW. PETUNIA WAS SITTING ON A WHITE DAISY. PATRICK WAS RESTING HIS LEGS ON A JUICY TOMATO. AND LUCY WAS MUNCHING ON A YELLOW-COLORED ROSE. HE THOUGHT HOW LUCKY HE WAS TO HAVE SUCH GREAT FRIENDS. YOU MIGHT BE WONDERING ABOUT THESE MISFITS, OR YOU MAY HAVE GUESSED ALREADY THAT THEY ARE ALL BUGS.

AS BENJAMIN, THE ANT, WONDERED ABOUT WHAT THE DAY'S ADVENTURE WOULD BE,
THE BRANCH OF THE MAPLE TREE BEGAN TO SHAKE. HE DUG HIS LITTLE CLAWS
INTO THE WOOD AS HE HEARD SOMETHING COMING UP BEHIND HIM. HE
REALIZED IT WAS THE THUMPING OF TINY SHOES BELONGING TO CHARLIE,
THE CENTIPEDE. BENJAMIN MOVED QUICKLY TO THE LEFT TO AVOID GETTING RUN OVER.
CHARLIE WAS FULL OF ENERGY. HE COULD NOT SIT OR STAND STILL LONG
ENOUGH TO HAVE A CONVERSATION. HE ALWAYS SEEMED TO BE IN A BIG HURRY.

AS CHARLIE RAN BY, BENJAMIN YELLED TO HIM, "HEY! WHAT HAPPENED TO YOUR FEET?"

BENJAMIN WAS LAUGHING AS CHARLIE SHARPLY MADE A TURN AND RAN THE OTHER
WAY PAST HIM. "IT LOOKS LIKE A RAINBOW EXPLODED ON YOUR FEET," BENJAMIN JOKED
AS CHARLIE RAN BY.

"WELL, YOU SEE," CHARLIE SAID, AS HE TRIED TO CATCH HIS BREATH.
"I WAS SO EXCITED THIS MORNING WHEN I WOKE UP, THAT I WAS NOT PAYING ATTENTION
TO THE SHOES I WAS PUTTING ON MY FEET. YOU KNOW BEN, WHEN YOU HAVE FIFTY
FEET AND YOU ARE IN A HURRY, YOU DON'T NOTICE."
BENJAMIN SMILED AND LAUGHED.

6

CHARLIE TURNED TO RUN THE OTHER WAY AGAIN. ALL BENJAMIN COULD SEE WERE CHARLIE'S EYES GLANCING AT HIM. HE DIDN'T HAVE TIME TO TURN HIS HEAD AS HE RAN BY.

"WHY ALL THE EXCITEMENT MY FRIEND?" HE ASKED THE YELLOW BLUR THAT SCURRIED BY.

"YOU SEE, I OVERHEARD," CHARLIE COULD BE HEARD SAYING. "THERE IS GOING TO BE A GREAT FEAST IN THE GARDEN TODAY. OH! OH! OH! I MUST GO NOW BEN. I WILL SEE YOU THERE."

THE YELLOW THREE-INCH SPEED DEMON TOOK OFF DOWN THE TREE IN A BLUR OF COLOR. BEN THOUGHT TO HIMSELF, "WHAT ON EARTH COULD THIS FEAST BE?" AND THEN WONDERED IF HE EVEN HEARD CHARLIE RIGHT. HE WAS MOVING FAST AND TALKING EVEN FASTER. HIS FRIENDS SOMETIMES HAD A TOUGH TIME HEARING HIM BECAUSE HE WAS ALWAYS MOVING AND TALKING SUPER-FAST.

8

BENJAMIN CONTINUED HIS MORNING WALK. SUDDENLY, HE STOPPED
LOSING HIS BALANCE AT THE END OF THE BRANCH. HE COULD NOT BELIEVE
WHAT HE WAS SEEING BELOW.

"IT'S SO BEAUTIFUL!" HE SAID OUT LOUD AS TEARS ROLLED
DOWN HIS LITTLE CHEEKS.

AS HE LOOKED DOWN ONTO THE FRESHLY MOWED GREEN
GRASS BELOW, THERE SAT THE MOST INCREDIBLE-LOOKING PICNIC HE HAD EVER SEEN.
ANTS LOVE PICNICS, AND HE HAD BEEN TO MANY, BUT THIS WAS THE BIGGEST
AND THE BEST HE'D EVER SEEN. IN THE CENTER OF THE BACKYARD, ON THE GRASS,
AMONGST THE TALL TREES AND COLORFUL FLOWERS, SAT A LARGE ORANGE AND BLUE
STRIPED BLANKET. THERE ON THAT BLANKET SAT THE MOST AMAZING FEAST EVER.
ONE PLATE HAD RED AND GREEN PERFECTLY CUT APPLES WITH PEANUT BUTTER.
THE OVAL-SHAPED BOWL TO IT'S LEFT HAD BRIGHT RED WATERMELON CUBES.
BEN'S MOUTH STARTED TO WATER. HE COULD BARELY CONTAIN HIS EXCITEMENT.

9

Happy Birthday To my
George

ON A YELLOW PLATTER SAT HAM AND CHEESE SANDWICHES WITH
THE MUSTARD DRIPPING OUT FROM BETWEEN THE BREAD. NEXT TO
THAT PLATTER WAS A PURPLE PLATE WITH JUMBO-SIZE CHOCOLATE CHIP COOKIES.
BENJAMIN COULD SMELL THE CHOCOLATE FROM THE BRANCH HE WAS STANDING ON.
HE ALMOST FELL OFF AT THE THOUGHT OF TAKING A BITE OUT OF THE COOKIES.
THEN IT HAPPENED. THE BACK DOOR OF THE SMALL WHITE HOUSE SUDDENLY
OPENED, AND THERE IT WAS. MRS. MILLER WAS CARRYING A LARGE, TALL,
FROSTED-COVERED CAKE. IT MUST HAVE BEEN TWO FEET TALL. IT HAD THICK
WHITE FROSTING WITH BLUE AND GREEN DECORATIONS. BENJAMIN COULD NOT
BELIEVE IT.   HIS ABSOLUTE FAVORITE WAS NOW MAKING ITS WAY TO
THE CENTER OF THE YARD.

AS THE LITTLE OLD LADY SHUFFLED TO THE PICNIC BLANKET, TRYING
CAREFULLY NOT TO DROP THE WORK OF ART, BEN BEGAN TO SHAKE
WITH EXCITEMENT. THEN HE HEARD HER. THE LITTLE WHITE-HAIRED
LADY WAS HUMMING A SWEET TUNE. HE THOUGHT HOW CUTE THE
LITTLE WOMAN LOOKED. SHE HAD HER LONG GRAY HAIR PULLED INTO
A BUN ON THE TOP OF HER HEAD. IT WAS WRAPPED WITH A LARGE
PURPLE RIBBON. SHE WAS WEARING A WHITE DRESS WITH
GREEN AND PURPLE POLKA DOTS. SHE WORE WHITE SHOES
WITH SHORT HEELS AS SHE ALWAYS DID, EVEN WHEN GARDENING.

BENJAMIN SCURRIED DOWN A BRANCH TO READ WHAT IT
SAID ON THE TOP OF THE CAKE.

"HAPPY BIRTHDAY TO MY GEORGE!" THE CAKE READ.

11

BENJAMIN QUICKLY TURNED TO HIS LEFT AS HE HEARD HAILEY, THE BUMBLE BEE, WHIZZING UP TO HIM.

"WHAT'S THE PLAN?" SHE ASKED AS SHE HOVERED OVER HIM. EVERYONE ALWAYS CAME TO HIM FOR ADVICE. HE ALWAYS LED HIS GROUP OF FRIENDS IN THEIR ADVENTURES, AND THIS WAS GOING TO BE A BIG ONE.

BENJAMIN THOUGHT FOR A SECOND. THEN, LOOKING AT THE BACK DOOR, HE SAW IT. HE REALIZED THEY MUST ACT FAST. THERE, STARING OUT AT THE GARDEN, WAS CHUBS THE CAT. HE WAS CLEANING HIS LONG BROWN WHISKERS AS HE KEPT AN EYE ON MRS. MILLER. BENJAMIN COULD TELL THAT THE CAT WAS EAGER TO GET BACK OUTSIDE AND MAKE HIMSELF AT HOME ON THE BLANKET. WHEN BENJAMIN WAS ABOUT TO GIVE HAILEY AN ANSWER, HE MADE EYE CONTACT WITH CHUBS. CHUBS SUDDENLY FROZE, HIS TAIL BEGAN TO TWITCH AS HE STARED AT THE TWO MISFITS HAVING A CONVERSATION. HE LET OUT A BIG MEOW AS THE ELDERLY LADY MADE HER WAY BACK INTO THE HOUSE.

"OH, HUSH MY SWEET BOY!" SHE SAID TO HIM AS SHE REACHED DOWN TO PAT THE TOP OF HIS FURRY HEAD. AS HE TRIED TO SCURRY OUT THE DOOR, SHE PUSHED HIM BACK WITH HER FOOT. "NOT TODAY, MY LOVE. IT'S GEORGE'S BIRTHDAY, AND WE ARE HAVING A PICNIC.   YOU NEED TO STAY IN THE HOUSE."

14

CHUBS RUBBED UP ON MRS. MILLER AND GAVE HER A SOFT MEOW BEFORE JUMPING ONTO THE TABLE TO LOOK OUT THE WINDOW. OF COURSE, HIS EYES WENT STRAIGHT TO BENJAMIN AND HAILEY.

"OH, YOU ARE SUCH A SWEET BOY!" THE LADY SAID TO THE OVERWEIGHT CAT. AS HE STOOD AT THE WINDOW STARING UP AT THE BUGS, THE LITTLE LADY KISSED HIM ON TOP OF HIS FURRY HEAD, "MOMMA LOVES HER BOY!"

CHUBS SAT AT THE WINDOW, STARING UP AT BENJAMIN AS HIS TAIL FLICKED BACK AND FORTH IN ANTICIPATION OF WHAT MIGHT BE COMING. HE WANTED TO GO OUTSIDE SO HE COULD CHASE THE LITTLE BUGS AROUND, BUT FOR NOW, HE WOULD HAVE TO WATCH FROM THE WINDOW. THE LITTLE LADY WALKED BACK OUTSIDE TO FINISH UP WITH THE FINAL DETAILS OF HER PICNIC.

BENJAMIN LOOKED AT HAILEY. "TELL EVERYONE TO MEET BY THE SUNFLOWERS IN TWO MINUTES," BEN SAID. HE WATCHED AS HAILEY BUZZED AWAY TO FIND THEIR FRIENDS. HE BEGAN TO THINK ABOUT THE FEAST THEY WERE ABOUT TO HAVE.

16

YOU ARE PROBABLY WONDERING WHY THIS GROUP OF FRIENDS CALL THEMSELVES MISFITS.
WELL, YOU SEE, THEY EACH HAVE SOMETHING THAT MAKES THEM DIFFERENT.

BENJAMIN THE ANT WAS BORN WITH ONLY ONE EYE.
HIS FAMILY TREATS HIM LIKE A BABY. THEY LEAVE HIM AT HOME A LOT,
WHICH MAKES HIM SAD. HIS MOM MADE HIM A BRIGHT YELLOW EYE
PATCH TO COVER WHERE HIS EYE WAS SUPPOSED TO BE. BENJAMIN
LOVES IT AND THINKS HE IS A PIRATE.

HAILEY THE BUMBLE BEE WANTS TO BE LIKED.
SINCE HUMANS ARE AFRAID OF BEES, WHEN SHE FLIES AROUND, PEOPLE
SWAT AT HER BECAUSE THEY FEAR SHE WILL STING THEM. ALL SHE WANTS
IS TO HAVE FRIENDS. SHE EVEN WEARS A BIG PINK BOW IN HOPES
THAT PEOPLE WILL LIKE HER. BUT NO ONE EVER GETS CLOSE ENOUGH TO SEE IT.

THEN THERE IS PETUNIA, THE BUTTERFLY. SHE HAS ONE WING SMALLER
THAN THE OTHER. WHEN SHE FLIES, SHE CAN ONLY GO A SHORT DISTANCE
BEFORE FLYING IN A CIRCLE. BENJAMIN FOUND HER CRYING IN THE GARDEN
ONE DAY BECAUSE HER FAMILY HAD FLOWN OFF AND DIDN'T REALIZE SHE
GOT LEFT BEHIND.

BENJAMIN AND PETUNIA ARE NOW BEST FRIENDS.

18

PATRICK, THE GRASSHOPPER, WAS BORN WITH A MISSING LEG, SO ALL HE CAN DO IS
WALK AROUND THE GARDEN DODGING THE HUMANS. HE CAN'T JUMP AND
FLY LIKE ALL HIS FAMILY. WITH ONLY ONE GOOD JUMPING LEG,
HE CAN NEVER JUMP FAST AND HIGH ENOUGH TO USE HIS WINGS.
HE IS STUCK WALKING AROUND AND WATCHING EVERYONE ELSE.
HIS BEST FRIEND IS ANGELINA, THE SPIDER.
SHE REALIZED ONE DAY THAT INSTEAD OF SPINNING BEAUTIFUL
WEBS, SHE ONLY CREATES BRIGHT GREEN ONES. HER SISTERS LAUGH AT HER,
SO SHE ONLY SPINS WEBS WHERE NO ONE ELSE CAN SEE THEM.
SHE WATCHES OVER PATRICK NOW TO MAKE SURE HE DOESN'T GET HURT.

THEN THERE IS SWEET LUCY, THE LADYBUG. LUCY WAS BORN WITHOUT THE BIG
BLACK SPOTS THAT HER ENTIRE FAMILY HAS. HER DAD WAS VERY EMBARRASSED
BY HER AND BANISHED HER FROM THE FAMILY. PETUNIA, THE BUTTERFLY,
FOUND LUCY ONE DAY SITTING UPON A LARGE YELLOW ROSE IN
THE MILLER'S YARD. LUCY HAD BIG TEARS RUNNING DOWN
HER CUTE LITTLE FACE. WHEN LUCY TOLD PETUNIA THE STORY, SHE KNEW
SHE WOULD FIT IN WITH ALL THE MISFITS.

WE CAN'T FORGET CHARLIE, THE CENTIPEDE. HE IS THE BEST FRIEND TO
ALL THE MISFITS. HE KEEPS EVERYONE LAUGHING AND RUNNING
AROUND WITH HIS ENERGY.

ALL THE BUGS ARE JUST ONE BIG HAPPY FAMILY.
THEY LIVE TOGETHER IN THIS BIG, COLORFUL, PEACEFUL GARDEN, WATCHING
OVER EACH OTHER AND HAVING FUN. THIS IS HOW ALL THE MISFITS BECAME FRIENDS.
THEY ARE ALL DIFFERENT AND UNUSUAL FROM OTHERS.
BUT TO EACH ONE OF THEM, THEY ARE PERFECT.

BENJAMIN WAITED AS THE GROUP GATHERED BELOW THE FLOWERS. AS THEY SAT
UNDER THE TALL BRIGHT SUNFLOWERS THAT GENTLY SWAYED IN THE WIND,
THEY DISCUSSED THEIR PLAN. THEY WOULD WORK IN TEAMS
OF TWO; EACH PAIR HAVING ONE TO TWO PLATES TO GET SAMPLES
FROM. PATRICK WOULD BE THEIR WATCH, JUST IN CASE OTHER BUGS
SHOWED UP AND TRIED TO TAKE OVER. MR. AND MRS. MILLER WERE
STILL INSIDE THE HOUSE, AND THE MISFITS HAD NO TIME TO WASTE.

THEY WAITED IN THEIR ASSIGNED SPOTS, WATCHING FOR PATRICK TO GIVE
THE OKAY.

SUDDENLY, OUT OF NOWHERE, THE WIND BEGAN TO BLOW. THE MISFITS GLANCED
UP INTO THE SKY. THAT IS WHEN THEY NOTICED THE SKY WAS CHANGING.
THE WHITE, PUFFY CLOUDS WERE NOW GRAY, AND THUNDER COULD
BE HEARD FAINTLY IN THE DISTANCE.

"OH NO!" BENJAMIN SAID.

Happy Birthday to my
George
24

THE NEXT THING THEY HEARD WAS PATRICK YELLING, "MOVE!" HE KNEW IF
THEY DIDN'T START NOW, THEY WOULD GET NOTHING.

ALL THE MISFITS SCATTERED TO THE BLANKET,
SPREADING OUT TO THE YUMMY, FILLED PLATES.

BEN AND ANGELINA WENT STRAIGHT FOR THE TALL BIRTHDAY CAKE.
EACH CRAWLED TO THE PLATE AND GRABBED
UP LARGE CRUMBS. HAILEY AND PETUNIA QUICKLY FLEW
TO THE PLATE OF CHOCOLATE CHIP COOKIES, EACH TAKING
LARGE BITES TO BRING THEM BACK TO THEIR FRIENDS.
CHARLIE AND LUCY WORKED TOGETHER TO PLACE A LARGE SLICE OF
THE SANDWICH ON CHARLIE'S BACK. THEY WOULD TAKE IT BACK
TO THE SUNFLOWERS, THEN QUICKLY GO BACK FOR MORE.
THE MISFITS WORKED FAST. LITTLE BENJAMIN
HAD DROPLETS OF SWEAT BEADING ON HIS FOREHEAD.   LUCY WAS OUT
OF BREATH TRYING TO PLACE THE LARGE BITS OF SANDWICH ON CHARLIE.
THEY GATHERED MORE AND MORE. THE PILE OF FOOD BEGAN
TO STACK UNDER THE SUNFLOWERS, THEN IT HAPPENED.

Happy Birthday To my

"THEY ARE COMING," WAS ALL THEY HEARD FROM PATRICK.

EACH BUG TOOK COVER. BENJAMIN HID UNDER THE PLATE THAT HELD THE BIG CAKE.
HAILEY, PETUNIA, AND LUCY FLEW TO THE FLOWERS SITTING IN A SMALL
VASE ON THE PICNIC BLANKET. PATRICK JUMPED ON ANGELINA'S BACK,
AND THEY TOOK OFF TOWARDS THE BASE OF THE TREE WITH CHARLIE
FOLLOWING BEHIND. ALL THE MISFITS FROZE AS THE HUMANS QUICKLY
BEGAN TO PICK UP THE FOOD. MR. MILLER GRABBED THE SANDWICHES
AND THE COOKIES. MRS. MILLER GRABBED THE FRUIT, AND THEY BOTH
WALKED BACK TO THEIR HOUSE, SLIPPING OUT OF SIGHT.

"WHAT'S GOING ON?" CHARLIE YELLED, LOOKING UP AT PATRICK.
"WHY ARE THEY TAKING THE FOOD INSIDE?"

"I DON'T KNOW WHY!" PATRICK SAID WITH CONFUSION
IN HIS VOICE. HE WAS LOOKING ALL AROUND THE YARD
TRYING TO FIGURE IT OUT.

28

THEN THEY FELT IT. LARGE DROPS OF WATER WERE FALLING FROM THE SKY.
IT WAS STARTING TO RAIN, AND IT WAS COMING FAST.
THE GROUP MOVED AS FAST AS THEY COULD TO THE SUNFLOWERS,
EACH GRABBING WHAT THEY COULD AND MOVING THEIR FEAST
INTO THE HOLE AT THE BASE OF THE OLD MAPLE TREE.
BUT SOMETHING WAS WRONG, SOMEONE WAS MISSING.

"WHERE IS BENJAMIN?" LUCY YELLED AS THE THUNDER ROLLED IN.
"WHERE DID HE GO?"

"I NEVER SAW HIM COME OUT FROM UNDERNEATH THE CAKE,"
PETUNIA SAID. BUT IT WAS DIFFICULT TO HEAR HER WITH THE
SOUND OF RAIN AND NOW THE WIND.

IN UNISON THEY ALL LOOKED TOWARDS THE TALL CAKE, NOW GETTING HIT WITH RAINDROPS. MRS. MILLER WAS PICKING UP THE CAKE WITH HER TINY LITTLE HANDS AND WAS WALKING IT TOWARDS THE HOUSE. BENJAMIN WAS STANDING AT THE EDGE OF THE PLATE WITH A LARGE PIECE OF CAKE IN HIS MOUTH, EYES OPENED WIDE WITH FEAR, LOOKING DOWN AT HIS FRIENDS, AS HE WAS BEING CARRIED AWAY INTO THE HUMAN'S HOUSE. HIS FRIENDS MOVED AWAY FROM THE TREE AS THE DOOR CLOSED, TRAPPING BENJAMIN INSIDE WITH THE COUPLE AND CHUBS, THE CAT.

"WHAT DO WE DO?" LUCY BEGAN TO CRY.

"WE NEED TO GET HIM OUT OF THERE, BEFORE THEY HURT HIM!" PETUNIA YELLED.

"OKAY! OKAY! OKAY!" CHARLIE BEGAN TO STUTTER.
"L- L- L- LET'S FIGURE THIS OUT."

Happy Birthday to my
George

THEY ALL STOOD BENEATH THE TREE, TRYING TO KEEP FROM GETTING HIT WITH RAIN.
THEY WOULD TAKE TURNS GLANCING UP AT THE HOUSE WINDOW.
THEY COULD SEE MR. AND MRS. MILLER SITTING AT THE KITCHEN TABLE NOW.
THEY WERE EATING SANDWICHES AND APPLES. THEY NOTICED THE CAKE
WAS SITTING ON THE COUNTER, UNTOUCHED.

AS SOON AS BENJAMIN HAD REALIZED HE WAS BEING TAKEN INTO THE HOUSE,
HE HID BACK UNDER THE BIRTHDAY CAKE. AS SOON AS THE PLATE WAS SET
DOWN ON THE COUNTER, AND HE SAW THE COUPLE AT THE TABLE,
HE QUICKLY CRAWLED OFF THE PLATE, ONTO THE COUNTER, AND UNDER THE BREADBOX.
HE WAITED, BUT REALIZED THAT THE HUMANS WERE NOT GOING TO BE HIS
PROBLEM; IT WAS THE BIG FLUFFY CAT THAT SAW HIM CRAWL OFF THE PLATE AND
TO THE BOX.   CHUBS, THE CAT, WAS NOW MAKING HIS WAY SLOWLY ACROSS THE KITCHEN
FLOOR TO SIT BELOW THE BREAD BOX.
WHEN CHUBS THOUGHT THAT THE COUPLE WAS NOT LOOKING, HE JUMPED UP ONTO THE
COUNTER, PLACING HIS FURRY BODY RIGHT IN FRONT OF THE BREADBOX. BEN BACKED
UP AS FAR AS HE COULD, SHAKING NERVOUSLY, WAITING FOR THE CAT TO EAT HIM.

"NOW, THERE OLD MAN," MRS. MILLER SAID TO HER CAT. "DON'T BE NAUGHTY."
SHE STOOD UP AND MOVED TOWARDS THE FURRY CRITTER WHO
WAS MAKING HIMSELF COMFORTABLE ON THE KITCHEN COUNTER.
SHE SCOOPED UP THE OVERWEIGHT FELINE AND GENTLY CARRIED HIM
BACK TO THE KITCHEN TABLE, AND SAT DOWN NEXT TO HER HUSBAND.

33

Birthday to my
George
34

"GEORGE, I TELL YOU. OUR BOY HAS A MIND OF HIS OWN." SHE SAID TO THE BALDING MAN.
"HE IS BECOMING MORE AND MORE MISCHIEVOUS EACH DAY."

"I KNOW MOMMA," THE MAN SAID BACK. "BUT HE IS OUR BABY BOY,
AND YOU LOVE HIM."

CHUBS LET OUT A PURR, RUBBING HIS HEAD, AGAINST THE LADY'S POLKA-DOTTED DRESS.
SHE LOOKED DOWN AT HIM, KISSING HIM ON HIS FURRY FACE.

"THAT I DO PAPA," SHE SAID TO MR. MILLER, NOW LOOKING AT HER
NINETY-YEAR-OLD HUSBAND ADORINGLY. "ARE YOU READY FOR SOME CAKE?"

"THAT SOUNDS WONDERFUL MARTHA!" AS HE SMILED BACK AT HER. "A BIG PIECE
WITH LOTS OF FROSTING ON IT PLEASE."

"I KNOW WHAT YOU LIKE GEORGE," SHE LAUGHED.

35

36

JUST AS SHE STOOD UP AND SAT HER CAT DOWN, CHUBS LEAPED OFF THE CHAIR AND RAN BACK OVER TO THE COUNTER, JUMPING UP AGAIN, THIS TIME SMASHING HIS FACE INTO THE BROWN SQUARE BOX. BENJAMIN BACKED UP AS FAR AS HE COULD STARING BACK AT THE BALL OF FUR.

"NO! NO! CHUBS!" MRS. MILLER YELLED. "WHAT HAS GOTTEN INTO YOU?"

SHE WALKED OVER TO HIM, SCOOPED HIM UP ONCE MORE, AND THIS TIME CARRIED HIM INTO HER BEDROOM, SHUTTING THE DOOR. HE STARED AT THE LITTLE SCARED ANT WHILE MEOWING LOUDLY WITH DEFIANCE. THE LADY WITH THE GRAY HAIR JUST SHOOK HER HEAD.

AS ALL THE COMMOTION WAS GOING ON INSIDE THE TINY WHITE HOUSE, THE MISFITS WERE FIGURING OUT THEIR PLAN IN THE YARD. THE RAIN CONTINUED TO COME DOWN, AND THE THUNDER CONTINUED TO ROLL ABOVE THEIR HEADS. IT WAS TIME FOR ACTION. THEY NEEDED TO GET THEIR FRIEND OUT OF THE HOUSE AND OUTSIDE TO SAFETY. HAILEY, LUCY, AND ANGELINA WERE GOING INSIDE. THE REST OF THE MISFITS WERE GOING TO PERCH THEMSELVES OUTSIDE THE KITCHEN SCREEN DOOR.

38

AS BEN SAT ON THE KITCHEN COUNTER WATCHING THE OLD COUPLE EAT THE LARGE PIECES OF CAKE, HE GLANCED OVER TO THE SCREEN DOOR AND SAW THE GIRLS COMING INTO THE HOUSE THROUGH AN OPENING. HE PACED BACK AND FORTH AT THE EDGE OF THE COUNTER. THE OBVIOUS THING FOR THE ANT TO DO WAS TO CRAWL DOWN THE SIDE OF THE CUPBOARD AND OUT THE DOOR. BUT, WITH ONLY ONE GOOD EYE, THINGS LIKE THAT DIDN'T WORK OUT FOR HIM. HE HAD TO BE EXTRA CAREFUL. THE GIRLS KNEW THEY HAD TO HELP HIM GET DOWN OFF THE COUNTER SAFELY.

AS THE TRIO GOT INTO THE HOUSE, THEY GLANCED UP AT BENJAMIN, SMILED AND WAVED. ANGELINA IMMEDIATELY CRAWLED UP THE SIDE OF THE COUNTER, AS LUCY AND HAILEY KEPT AN EYE ON THE COUPLE AT THE TABLE. AS THE COUPLE FINISHED UP THEIR CAKE AND STARTED TO LOOK LIKE THEY WERE GOING TO GET UP, LUCY QUICKLY FLEW UP TO THE TABLE, LANDED ON MR. MILLER'S HAND, AND SAT QUIETLY.   THE COUPLE WAS STARTLED BY THE LADYBUG, BUT THEY LOVED THESE LITTLE ORANGE CRITTERS SO MUCH THAT THEY JUST STARED AT HER.

"OH, ISN'T THAT SWEET?" MRS. MILLER SAID TO HER HUSBAND. "WHAT A CUTE LITTLE BUG."

"SHE SURE IS HONEY," HE SAID AS HE WATCHED THE LITTLE BUG CRAWL UP TO HIS WRIST.

40

AS BOTH SAT STARING AT THE INSECT, THEY COULD HEAR A SCRATCH ON THE BEDROOM DOOR, THEN A DEEP MEOW. CHUBS KNEW WHAT WAS GOING ON, AND HE WANTED OUT, RIGHT NOW.

LUCY WAS STARTLED HEARING THE CAT BUT KEPT SITTING ON GEORGE'S HAND. SHE GLANCED OVER AND SAW HAILEY SITTING ON THE RIP IN THE SCREEN DOOR. SHE THEN LOOKED OVER AS SHE WATCHED ANGELINA SCURRY UP THE SIDE OF THE KITCHEN COUNTER, LIKE THE FAST LITTLE SPIDER SHE WAS, AND PLOP HERSELF DOWN NEXT TO BENJAMIN. ANGELLINA THEN STARTED TO SPIN ONE OF HER BRIGHT GREEN WEBS AS HE LOOKED ON. THE PLAN WAS WORKING. LUCY KEPT HER EYE ON THE TWO ON THE COUNTER AS THE MILLERS ADMIRED HER. THEN WHEN THE WEB WAS FINISHED, SHE WATCHED AS BENJAMIN CRAWLED ONTO ANGELINA'S BACK, AND THE TWO JUMPED OFF THE COUNTER. THE OLDER COUPLE WERE SO MESMERIZED BY LUCY AND HER CUTENESS, THAT THEY HAD NO IDEA WHAT WAS GOING ON.

LUCY AND HAILEY HELD THEIR BREATH AS THEY WAITED.

41

THE TWO FRIENDS JUMPED FROM THE COUNTER, THE GREEN PARACHUTE OPENED, AND BEN AND ANGELINA FLOATED DOWN TO THE FLOOR. AS THEY SOFTLY LANDED, HE CRAWLED OFF HER BACK, AND THEY BOTH STARTED TO MAKE THEIR WAY TO THE BACK DOOR. THEY WOULD QUICKLY CRAWL OUT UNDER THE DOOR, WHILE LUCY AND HAILEY WOULD LEAVE THROUGH THE OPENING IN THE SCREEN.

THEN IT HAPPENED. OUT OF NOWHERE, CHUBS CAME RUNNING DOWN THE HALLWAY AFTER ESCAPING THROUGH THE BATHROOM DOOR ATTACHED TO THE BEDROOM. MRS. MILLER HAD FORGOTTEN TO MAKE SURE IT WAS SHUT TIGHT. CHUBS WAS ABLE TO PUT HIS PAW UNDER THE DOOR AND LOOSEN IT UP ENOUGH FOR HIM TO ESCAPE. CHUBS BURST HIS WAY INTO THE KITCHEN AND SAW WHAT WAS GOING ON. ALL FOUR OF THE INSECTS FROZE.

43

44

MRS. MILLER JUMPED UP AS SHE SAW THE CAT RUNNING IN. THINKING HE WAS GOING TO JUMP BACK ON THE COUNTER, SHE TRIED TO SCOOP HIM UP. BUT SHE COULDN'T CATCH HIM. ANGELINA AND BENJAMIN RAN BEHIND THE REFRIGERATOR, JUST IN TIME TO MISS GETTING SMASHED AS CHUBS, OVERLY LARGE PAW CAME DOWN RIGHT BEHIND THEM. LUCY CONTINUED TO WATCH IN HORROR, UNCERTAIN OF WHAT TO DO. MR. MILLER JUST SAT AND WATCHED AS HIS WIFE TRIED TO CATCH THEIR FELINE CHILD.

HAILEY HAD TO DO SOMETHING. SHE HAD TO MAKE A DISTRACTION. SHE QUICKLY FLEW INTO THE KITCHEN, BUZZING AROUND MRS. MILLER'S HEAD. HER HUSBAND INSTANTLY STOOD UP, KNOCKING LUCY OFF HIS HAND AS HE TRIED TO SWAT THE BUMBLE BEE AWAY FROM HIS WIFE. LUCY, THE LADYBUG, QUICKLY FLEW AWAY FROM THE OLD MAN, OUT THE OPENING IN THE SCREEN DOOR, AND OUT TO SAFETY. SHE SAW HER OTHER FRIENDS SITTING AT THE WINDOW, STILL WATCHING IN FEAR.

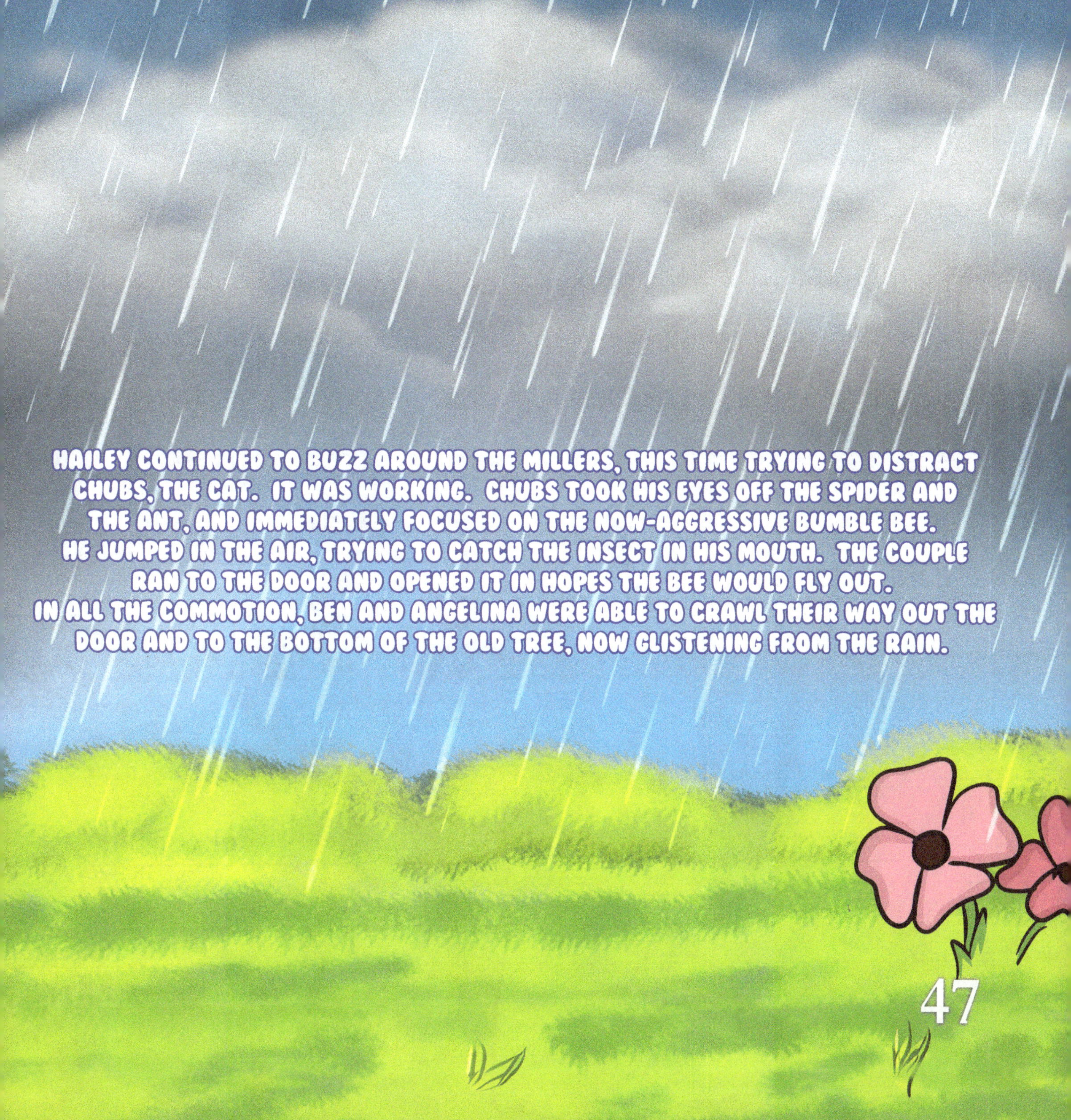
HAILEY CONTINUED TO BUZZ AROUND THE MILLERS, THIS TIME TRYING TO DISTRACT
CHUBS, THE CAT. IT WAS WORKING. CHUBS TOOK HIS EYES OFF THE SPIDER AND
THE ANT, AND IMMEDIATELY FOCUSED ON THE NOW-AGGRESSIVE BUMBLE BEE.
HE JUMPED IN THE AIR, TRYING TO CATCH THE INSECT IN HIS MOUTH. THE COUPLE
RAN TO THE DOOR AND OPENED IT IN HOPES THE BEE WOULD FLY OUT.
IN ALL THE COMMOTION, BEN AND ANGELINA WERE ABLE TO CRAWL THEIR WAY OUT THE
DOOR AND TO THE BOTTOM OF THE OLD TREE, NOW GLISTENING FROM THE RAIN.

HAILEY FLEW AROUND THE KITCHEN IN CIRCLES, AND WHEN SHE NOTICED THE OPEN DOOR, SHE QUICKLY FLEW TOWARDS IT AS CHUBS CHASED HER. AS HER LITTLE HEART BEAT FASTER, FEARING SHE MAY BE EATEN, SHE COULD SENSE CHUB'S APPROACH. JUST AS HE JUMPED IN THE AIR AND WAS ABOUT TO LAND ON THE LITTLE BEE, MRS. MILLER SCOOPED UP THE NAUGHTY KITTY AND SLAMMED THE DOOR, LOCKING THE CAT INSIDE. HAILEY FLEW TOWARDS THE TREE AS THE OTHER FRIENDS FOLLOWED BEHIND.

"WHAT AN EXCITING BIRTHDAY MOMMA!" THE OLD MAN COULD BE HEARD SAYING. THEY BOTH SAT DOWN AT THE TABLE AFTER MRS. MILLER PUT THE CAT ON THE FLOOR. "I COULD SURE USE SOME MORE CAKE."

"YOU EAT ALL THE CAKE YOU WANT TO MY LOVE," SHE SAID. "IT'S YOUR DAY!" SHE SMILED AT HIM AS IF THE CHAOS HADN'T OCCURRED.

THE OLDER COUPLE BOTH ENJOYED ANOTHER PIECE OF CAKE AS CHUBS SAT AT THE SCREEN DOOR STARING OUT INTO THE BACKYARD. THE MISFITS SAT UNDER THE TALL MAPLE TREE, ALL REUNITED, FEASTING ON WHAT THEY WERE ABLE TO GET BEFORE THE RAIN.

"WHAT A DAY!" BENJAMIN SAID TO HIS FRIENDS.

"YES, INDEED BEN," PATRICK MUMBLED THROUGH A MOUTHFUL OF SANDWICH CRUMBS.

THE MISFITS GLANCED TOWARDS THE LITTLE HOUSE AND THE SCREEN DOOR. THEY COULD SEE CHUBS STILL SITTING THERE STARING AT THEM. THEY SMILED AND WAVED AT HIM, THEIR LITTLE MOUTHS AND HANDS FULL OF GOODIES. CHUB'S TAIL TWITCHED, AND HIS LITTLE WHISKERS SHOOK. HE SMOOSHED HIS FACE TO THE SCREEN, WATCHING THE LITTLE BUGS EATING UNDER THE TREE. THE MISFITS SAT QUIETLY, EATING AND WONDERING WHAT THEIR NEXT ADVENTURE WOULD BE.